Frankenstein;

or, The Modern Prometheus

Lightbox Literature Studies

Katie Gillespie

LIGHTBOX
openlightbox.com

Go to **www.openlightbox.com** and enter this book's unique code.

ACCESS CODE

LBXH8496

Lightbox is an all-inclusive digital solution for the teaching and learning of curriculum topics in an original, groundbreaking way. Lightbox is based on National Curriculum Standards.

LIGHTBOX SUPPLEMENTARY RESOURCES

SHARE
Share titles within your Learning Management System (LMS) or Library Circulation System

CURRICULUM
Find national and state curriculum correlations

CITATION
Create bibliographical references following APA, CMOS, and MLA styles

STANDARD FEATURES OF LIGHTBOX

AUDIO High-quality narration using text-to-speech system

ACTIVITIES Printable PDFs that can be emailed and graded

SLIDESHOWS Pictorial overviews of key concepts

VIDEOS Embedded high-definition video clips

WEBLINKS Curated links to external, child-safe resources

TRANSPARENCIES Step-by-step layering of maps, diagrams, charts, and timelines

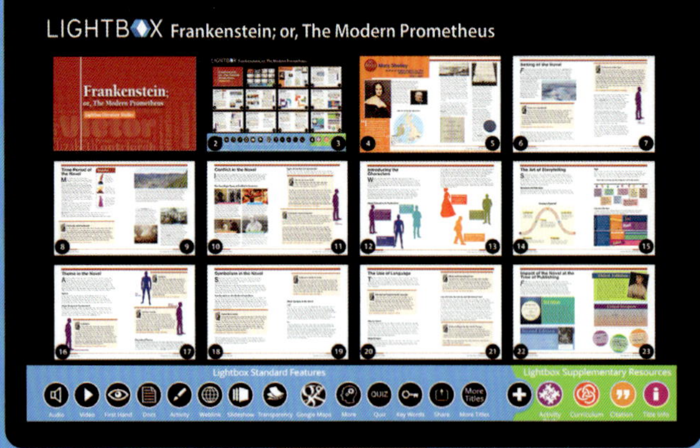

INTERACTIVE MAPS Interactive maps and aerial satellite imagery

QUIZZES Ten multiple-choice questions that are automatically graded and emailed for teacher assessment

KEY WORDS Matching key concepts to their definitions

Contents

2 Access Lightbox Student Edition

4 All About Mary Shelley

6 Setting of the Novel

8 Time Period of the Novel

10 Conflict in the Novel

12 Introducing the Characters

14 The Art of Storytelling

16 Theme in the Novel

18 Symbolism in the Novel

20 The Use of Language

22 Impact of the Novel at the Time of Publishing

24 Impact of the Novel Now

26 Perspectives on Scientific Discovery and the Pursuit of Knowledge

28 Writing a Comparative Essay

30 Key Words/Literary Terms

31 Index

32 Log on to www.openlightbox.com

EXTENSION ACTIVITY

Analyzing a Video

Students will watch and assess a video related to a component of the novel, and write an analysis of the video. An exemplary video analysis will meet the following criteria.

- Identifies the purpose of the video
- Identifies the intended audience of the video
- Describes how the content of the video is presented
- Summarizes the information and opinions presented in the video
- Analyzes the quality of the content presented in the video
- Assesses the effectiveness of the video
- Discusses the technical aspects of the video and whether or not these enhance the content
- Determines whether the images and graphics used in the video relate to the content
- Determines whether the video is easy to follow and understand
- Gives the analysis a clear and consistent purpose
- Organizes the analysis in a logical, effective manner
- Presents a strong, clear argument on the video
- Provides strong and accurate details to support the argument about the video
- Considers other perspectives on the purpose and effectiveness of the video
- Makes connections between claims and between the video and the novel
- Properly integrates quotations from the video
- Cites all sources used in the analysis

All About Mary Shelley

Author of *Frankenstein; or, The Modern Prometheus*

1797–1851

Mary Wollstonecraft Godwin was born on August 30, 1797, in London, England. Both of her parents were talented writers. Mary's father, William Godwin, was a political philosopher and journalist. His most well-known book is *Enquiry Concerning Political Justice, and Its Influences on Morals and Happiness*. Her mother, Mary Wollstonecraft, was an advocate for women's rights, best known for her work titled *A Vindication of the Rights of Woman*. However, Mary never knew her mother, as she died only 10 days after Mary was born.

"Invention, it must be humbly admitted, does not consist in creating out of void, but out of chaos; the materials must, in the first place, be afforded: it can give form to dark, shapeless substances, but cannot bring into being the substance itself."

Mary Wollstonecraft Shelley, Introduction to *Frankenstein,* October 15, 1831

MAP OF THE UNITED KINGDOM

Mary and her stepmother, Mary Jane Clairmont, did not get along, so when Mary was a teenager, she was sent to Scotland. During a visit home in 1812, she met Percy Bysshe Shelley, a young poet William was mentoring. Although he was married, Percy and Mary fell in love, and ran away together to travel Europe. In 1815, their first daughter was born, but only lived for a brief time. In 1816, Mary gave birth to a son, named William. That same year, the couple traveled to Geneva, Switzerland, where Mary began writing *Frankenstein*, a task she would finish in Bath. In October 1816, Mary's half-sister Fanny passed away, followed by Percy's wife Harriet in December. Percy and Mary were married soon after.

At the urging of her husband, Mary worked more on her novel, which was completed in 1817. In September that year, Mary gave birth to their third child, another daughter. In November, Percy and Mary published *History of a Six Weeks' Tour*, a **Romantic** travel narrative based on their trips in Europe. This was Mary's first published work. It was shortly followed by the publication of *Frankenstein*, on January 1, 1818.

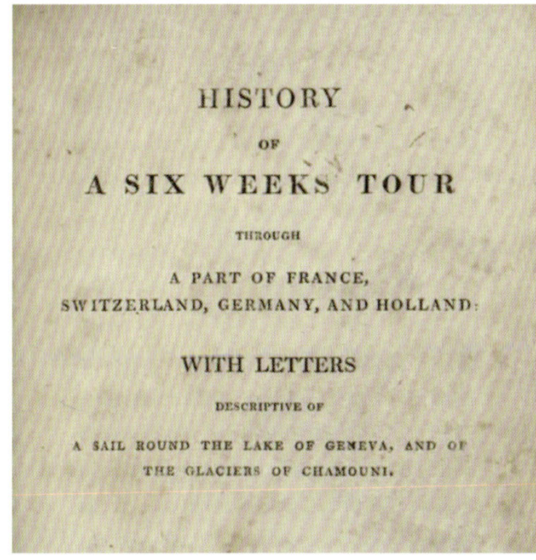

HISTORY

OF

A SIX WEEKS' TOUR

THROUGH

A PART OF FRANCE,
SWITZERLAND, GERMANY, AND HOLLAND:

WITH LETTERS

DESCRIPTIVE OF

A SAIL ROUND THE LAKE OF GENEVA, AND OF
THE GLACIERS OF CHAMOUNI.

In June 1819, the Shelleys' young son William passed away. That November, their fourth child was born, a son named Percy Florence. He would be the only Shelley child to survive to adulthood. After losing her daughter in June 1822, misfortune would soon befall Mary yet again in July, when her husband drowned during a storm while out sailing. Widowed and left to raise a young child alone, Mary continued her literary pursuits and was able to make a living.

Over the next two decades, Mary wrote several works of her own, including a revised edition of *Frankenstein* that was published in October 1831. She also edited the writings of both her husband and father. Although much of her life was filled with tragedy, Mary spent her later years with loved ones, passing away in London, England, at age 53. Her death is now thought to have been caused by a brain tumor. She was **interred** by her only living son, Sir Percy Florence Shelley, in the family vault at St. Peter's Church in Bournemouth, England.

TEACHER NOTES

Google Maps

Mary Shelley's House of Frankenstein, Bath, England

Using Google Street View, explore Bath, England, where Mary Shelley wrote much of her famous novel, and investigate the atmospheric attraction celebrating the *Frankenstein* author and her creation.

Video

Mary Shelley's Frankenstein 200 Year Anniversary

In this video, professor Leo Braudy examines the circumstances that led Mary Shelley to write *Frankenstein*.

1. How might Mary Shelley's life circumstances leading up to her writing *Frankenstein* have affected the course of the novel's narrative? Were these circumstances affecting her unique, or were they a product of her time? Why?
2. Braudy notes that *Frankenstein* is still relevant today when applied to concepts, such as cloning, that did not exist at the time in which the novel was written. Why might this be the case?

EXTENSION ACTIVITY

Researching for a Writing Assignment

Students will complete a thorough research process to prepare for a writing assignment, and organize their research in a logical manner that supports their writing. An exemplary research process will meet the following criteria.

- Creates a goal for the research, based on the topic and working thesis
- Creates specific, thoughtful, and inventive research questions that are relevant to the topic of the writing assignment
- Produces a list of categories, key words, and related ideas to effectively assist in researching
- Uses high-quality sources that pertain to the topic and come in a variety of formats, such as books, journals, primary sources, websites, and databases
- Determines the accuracy of all sources used
- Uses sources that provide balanced research and various perspectives on the topic in question
- Takes notes to highlight the key facts and ideas in order to answer all research questions
- Extracts relevant, detailed information from the sources during the note-taking process
- Organizes the research notes in a clear and concise manner
- Organizes the research notes logically and in a way that sets up the information and ideas for analysis and the writing process
- Analyzes the information and produces ideas and points to support the working thesis
- Uses an effective and suitable format to present all research
- Properly cites all sources used

Setting of the Novel

Frankenstein features multiple settings. The novel begins in **epistolary** form, with explorer Robert Walton, who is attempting to sail to the North Pole, writing to his sister Margaret. Walton's first letter to Margaret comes from St. Petersburg, Russia, and his second is sent from Archangel, also in Russia. By the time Walton writes his third and fourth letters, he has traveled farther on his voyage, and his ship is surrounded by large sheets of ice. It is here that he meets the title character, Victor Frankenstein, who begins to tell Walton the story of his life. Victor reveals that he was born in Naples, Italy, but his family is from Geneva, Switzerland. Frankenstein talks about his childhood, followed by his move to Ingolstadt, Germany, where he attended university.

Geneva to Ingolstadt

When I had attained the age of seventeen, my parents resolved that I should become a student at the university of Ingolstadt. I had hitherto attended the schools of Geneva, but my father thought it necessary for the completion of my education that I should be made acquainted with other customs than those of my native country. My departure was therefore fixed at an early date, but before the day resolved upon could arrive, the first misfortune of my life occurred—an omen, as it were, of my future misery.

Victor Frankenstein, Volume One, Chapter 3, First Edition

While in Ingolstadt, Frankenstein creates the Monster from pieces of dead bodies. However, he rejects his creation and the monster disappears shortly afterwards. Frankenstein is planning a trip back home when he receives a letter from his father, notifying him of the death of his youngest brother William, the Monster's first victim. The story then follows Frankenstein back to Geneva until he meets the Monster again, in the Alps mountains.

TEACHER NOTES

A Monster in the Alps

From the side where I now stood Montanvert was exactly opposite, at the distance of a league; and above it rose Mont Blanc, in awful majesty. I remained in a recess of the rock, gazing on this wonderful and stupendous scene. The sea, or rather the vast river of ice, wound among its dependent mountains, whose aerial summits hung over its recesses. Their icy and glittering peaks shone in the sunlight over the clouds.…I suddenly beheld the figure of a man, at some distance, advancing towards me with superhuman speed. He bounded over the crevices in the ice, among which I had walked with caution; his stature, also, as he approached, seemed to exceed that of man.

Victor Frankenstein, Volume Two, Chapter 2, First Edition

Here, the creature takes over the narrative, recounting his time in rural Germany and demanding that Frankenstein make him a female partner. The story shifts its **perspective** back to Frankenstein, who returns to Geneva, then journeys to London, England, with his friend Henry Clerval. After months there, the pair decide to go to Scotland, then part ways. Frankenstein travels alone to the Orkney Islands, where he starts to make his second creature.

The Monster reappears, and upon seeing him, Frankenstein destroys the female creation. In retaliation, the Monster threatens Victor and kills Clerval. Although he is suspected of Henry's murder, Frankenstein is found to be innocent, then returns to Geneva with his father and marries his beloved, Elizabeth. However, the Monster kills Elizabeth and Victor's father dies of grief soon after.

Now completely alone in the world, Frankenstein vows to destroy the Monster, which leads him to the Arctic. There, he encounters Walton and tells him the tragic tale. Having come full circle, the novel ends with a return to epistolary form, as Walton takes over once again and finishes the story through his letters to Margaret.

Victor Frankenstein

Weblink

The Real-Life Places That Inspired *Frankenstein*

This article from *Smithsonian Magazine* details Mary Shelley's inspirations for the settings of *Frankenstein.*

1. How do the novel's multiple settings relate to the relationship between Victor Frankenstein and the Monster? Why is this important?
2. Which of the novel's settings contribute to a theme of "sublime nature?" How? In what ways do these settings support the idea that nature is both beautiful and dangerous? What are the consequences of disrespecting nature?

EXTENSION ACTIVITY

Creating a Podcast

Students will research an event that took place between the late 1700s and early 1800s. Then, they will communicate their research and make connections to the novel by creating a podcast. An exemplary podcast will meet the following criteria.

- Begins with an engaging introduction to grab the listener's attention
- Demonstrates thorough knowledge of the topic
- Demonstrates understanding of the purpose of the podcast
- Presents information with the target audience in mind
- Focuses on a specific, narrow topic
- Uses accurate, specific, high-quality facts and details in the podcast
- Organizes and presents the main points and supporting facts in a logical, effective manner
- Establishes a clear purpose to the podcast immediately
- Identifies the speaker and the location and date the podcast was produced
- Uses vocabulary that enhances the content of the podcast
- Uses correct grammar throughout the podcast
- Maintains focus on the main topic throughout the podcast
- Clearly summarizes the main argument in the conclusion of the podcast
- Delivers the podcast in a well-rehearsed, conversational manner
- Enunciates clearly and with engaging rhythm and expression
- Edited to a length that will keep the listener engaged
- Uses audio effects in an effective manner to enhance the podcast
- Recorded in a quiet environment free of background noises

Time Period of the Novel

Mary Wollstonecraft Godwin began writing *Frankenstein* during the summer of 1816. At the time, she was traveling in Switzerland with Percy Bysshe Shelley. The couple often spent their evenings reading ghost stories with friends, including British poet George Gordon Byron, commonly referred to as Lord Byron. One night, Byron proposed a competition in which each writer would create their own ghost story. Mary came up with a short, horrifying tale. It was Percy who encouraged Mary to develop the story further. She finished writing it in 1817, and the novel was published the following year.

Although *Frankenstein* was written in the early 1800s, it is set in the 1700s. No specific years are given in the text, but Walton's letters are dated "17—." The most likely time period is somewhere near the end of the 18th century, indicated by references to electricity and **galvanism** in the novel. Given that scientist Luigi Galvani's discovery of galvanism occurred on September 20, 1786, this puts the events of the story sometime after that, but before the beginning of the 19th century.

Snapshot

Mary was only 18 years old when she started writing *Frankenstein*.

Due to the eruption of Mount Tambora, 1816 is known as the "Year without a Summer."

Of the four people that participated in Byron's contest, Mary was the only one to complete her story.

Electricity and Galvanism

By one of those caprices of the mind, which we are perhaps most subject to in early youth, I at once gave up my former occupations; set down natural history and all its progeny as a deformed and abortive creation; and entertained the greatest disdain for a would-be science, which could never even step within the threshold of real knowledge. In this mood of mind I betook myself to the mathematics, and the branches of study appertaining to that science, as being built upon secure foundations, and so worthy of my consideration.

Victor Frankenstein, Volume One, Chapter 2, First Edition

Comparing Victor Frankenstein and the Monster

Frankenstein

Physical Description
- Is often described as ill
- His body is emaciated
- His eyes have an expression of wildness or even madness

Personality
- Ambitious
- Curious
- Arrogant
- Selfish
- Obsessive
- Single-minded

Place in the World
- The protagonist of the novel
- Is raised in Geneva, Switzerland
- Takes an interest in the work of Cornelius Agrippa
- Attends university in Ingolstadt, Germany, where he studies natural science
- Follows the Monster to the Arctic

Relationships
- Creator of the Monster
- Eldest son of Caroline Beaufort and Alphonse Frankenstein
- Brother of Ernest and William Frankenstein
- Eventual husband of Elizabeth Lavenza
- Best friend of Henry Clerval

Motivation and Behavior
- Driven by his desire to discover the secret of life
- Abandons his creation, who he treats with fear, disgust, and hatred
- Is overcome with guilt and shame, but refuses to tell anyone about the Monster
- Swears to destroy the Monster, who has taken away everyone he loves

Monster

Place in the World
- The antagonist of the novel
- Has no past or family history
- Attempts to integrate into society, but is shunned because of his grotesque appearance
- Travels throughout Europe before fleeing to the Arctic

Motivation and Behavior
- Starts with the mind of a young child, but learns to speak eloquently and acquires rational thought and emotions
- Starts out wanting to be loved and accepted, but becomes isolated and angry due to the prejudice of those he encounters
- Seeks vengeance upon his creator after being denied a mate

Physical Description
- 8 feet (2.4 meters) tall and enormously strong
- Assembled from various body parts
- Hideously ugly
- Has dull, watery eyes, lustrous black hair, a shriveled complexion, yellow skin, black lips, and pearly white teeth

Relationships
- Created by Victor Frankenstein
- Murderer of William Frankenstein, Henry Clerval, and Elizabeth Lavenza
- Indirectly causes the deaths of Justine Moritz and Alphonse Frankenstein
- Tries to connect with De Lacey, but is attacked by Felix and later burns down the family's cottage

Personality
- Sensitive
- Gentle
- Kind
- Bitter
- Lonely
- Vengeful

Transparency–Chart

Questions for Character Analysis

Analyze how specific character features, such as conflicts, motivations, relationships, place in the world, and personality affect the plot of *Frankenstein*. Cite strong and thorough textual evidence to support your analysis of what the novel says explicitly as well as the inferences you may have drawn from the novel's setting, themes, and symbols.

Quiz Answers

1. D
2. D
3. B
4. C
5. A
6. C
7. D
8. A
9. A
10. C

Key Words

anesthetic: a substance that makes someone unable to feel pain

apartheid: the segregation of and discrimination against the non-white majority in the Republic of South Africa

BAFTA: the British Academy of Film and Television Arts, an organization that supports the arts in the United Kingdom

enlightenment: being aware and well-informed

epistolary: relating to or consisting of letters

galvanism: a scientific theory that electric currents result in life

interred: placed in a grave or tomb

morality: a belief system based on principles of what is right and wrong, and using this system to make decisions based on ethics and doing the right thing

pathogens: germs or viruses that cause diseases

perspective: a certain point of view or position regarding a subject

prejudice: a preconceived opinion or idea formed without reason or sufficient knowledge

revolution: the generally violent overthrow of a government or ruler in an effort to put a new one into power

Romantic: relating to an 18th-century movement focused on the imagination and emotions

society: an organized community of people interacting with each other

sublime: grand, supreme, or awe-inspiring

universal: common to all cases; present or appearing in all conditions

vaccination: a substance put into someone's body to help prevent disease

values: an individual's standards of behavior and what aspects of life they consider to be most important

Literary Terms

action: everything that occurs in a narrative

allusion: to suggest or hint at a subject

antagonist: the character who stands in opposition to the protagonist; in some cases, the antagonist creates or represents the conflict that the protagonist faces

characteristics: identifying features or qualities belonging typically to a person, place, or thing

climax: the moment of greatest tension in the story's action

conflict: a struggle between two or more opposing forces, creating a tension that must be resolved

dialogue: the spoken conversations that the characters have with each other

exposition: the beginning of the story, where the characters and setting are introduced

falling action: the events that take place after the climax, leading up to the end of the story

Freytag's Pyramid: a narrative structure consisting of five elements; this includes exposition, rising action, climax, falling action, and resolution

imagery: the use of figurative language to describe certain things in a way that appeals to the reader's senses

mood: the overall feeling that the narrative is intended to evoke within the reader

narrative: a logically arranged series of events presented for an audience; a story

personify: to give human traits or a personal nature to a non-human concept or object

plot: the specific action that propels a story forward

protagonist: the central character in a piece of fiction who must deal with a conflict and often undergoes some type of change as a result

resolution: the end of the story, when the problems are resolved and the action comes to a conclusion

rising action: the events that create increased drama or tension

simile: a comparison of two different things using "like" or "as"

style: the unique way that writers use language to tell their story; this can include word choice, the use of imagery, and the length and organization of sentences

symbolism: a stylistic device using symbols to represent and intensify concepts and ideas

theme: the underlying topic, idea, or position in a work that is often a general, universal statement about life

voice: a writer's distinct personality and form of expression, as shown through his or her written work

EXTENSION ACTIVITY

Analyzing a Video

Students will watch and assess a video related to a component of the novel, and write an analysis of the video. An exemplary video analysis will meet the following criteria.

- Identifies the purpose of the video
- Identifies the intended audience of the video
- Describes how the content of the video is presented
- Summarizes the information and opinions presented in the video
- Analyzes the quality of the content presented in the video
- Assesses the effectiveness of the video
- Discusses the technical aspects of the video and whether or not these enhance the content
- Determines whether the images and graphics used in the video relate to the content
- Determines whether the video is easy to follow and understand
- Gives the analysis a clear and consistent purpose
- Organizes the analysis in a logical, effective manner
- Presents a strong, clear argument on the video
- Provides strong and accurate details to support the argument about the video
- Considers other perspectives on the purpose and effectiveness of the video
- Makes connections between claims and between the video and the novel
- Properly integrates quotations from the video
- Cites all sources used in the analysis

All About Mary Shelley

Author of *Frankenstein; or, The Modern Prometheus*

1797–1851

Mary Wollstonecraft Godwin was born on August 30, 1797, in London, England. Both of her parents were talented writers. Mary's father, William Godwin, was a political philosopher and journalist. His most well-known book is *Enquiry Concerning Political Justice, and Its Influences on Morals and Happiness*. Her mother, Mary Wollstonecraft, was an advocate for women's rights, best known for her work titled *A Vindication of the Rights of Woman*. However, Mary never knew her mother, as she died only 10 days after Mary was born.

> "Invention, it must be humbly admitted, does not consist in creating out of void, but out of chaos; the materials must, in the first place, be afforded: it can give form to dark, shapeless substances, but cannot bring into being the substance itself."
>
> Mary Wollstonecraft Shelley, Introduction to *Frankenstein*, October 15, 1831

MAP OF THE UNITED KINGDOM

Contents

2 Access Lightbox Student Edition
4 All About Mary Shelley
6 Setting of the Novel
8 Time Period of the Novel
10 Conflict in the Novel
12 Introducing the Characters
14 The Art of Storytelling
16 Theme in the Novel
18 Symbolism in the Novel
20 The Use of Language
22 Impact of the Novel at the Time of Publishing
24 Impact of the Novel Now
26 Perspectives on Scientific Discovery and the Pursuit of Knowledge
28 Writing a Comparative Essay
30 Key Words/Literary Terms
31 Index
32 Log on to www.openlightbox.com

Index

Adam 17, 18, 19
Alps 6, 7, 17
ambition 12, 16, 26, 27, 29
Archangel 6
A Vindication of the Rights of Woman 4

Bath, England 4, 24
Beaufort, Caroline 29
Bournemouth, England 4, 5
Bride of Frankenstein 24
Byron, George Gordon 8

Clairmont, Mary Jane 5
Clerval, Henry 7, 13, 15, 29
conflict 10, 11, 12, 13, 14

De Lacey 19, 29

electricity 8
Enquiry Concerning Political Justice, and Its Influences on Morals and Happiness 4

fire 18, 19
Frankenstein (film) 24
Frankenstein (television mini-series) 25
Frankenstein, Alphonse 13, 29
Frankenstein, Ernest 29
Frankenstein Revived 25
Frankenstein, Victor 6, 7, 8, 11, 12, 13, 15, 16, 17, 18, 19, 20, 21, 23, 24, 25, 26, 27, 29
Frankenstein, William 6, 13, 25, 29
Frankenweenie 24
French Revolution 9

galvanism 8
Geneva, Switzerland 5, 6, 7, 29
Godwin, William 4, 5, 22
gothic 22

Industrial Revolution 9
Ingolstadt, Germany 6, 29
isolation 16, 17

knowledge 8, 9, 17, 18, 19, 26, 27

Lavenza, Elizabeth 7, 13, 15, 23, 29
Les Misérables 10
letters 6, 7, 8, 12, 15, 21
light 9, 11, 18, 19
literary devices 14, 15, 20
London, England 4, 5, 7, 24, 25
loss of innocence 17

Mary Shelley's Frankenstein 24, 25
Monster 6, 7, 9, 11, 12, 13, 15, 16, 17, 18, 19, 21, 24, 25, 26, 29
Mont Blanc 7
Moritz, Justine 29
Mount Tambora 8, 9

Naples, Italy 6
North Pole 6, 19

Orkney Islands 7

prejudice 17, 29
Presumption; or The Fate of Frankenstein 23
Prometheus 18, 19

revenge 11, 12, 17, 29
Royal National Theatre 25

science fiction 22, 25
Shelley, Mary (Wollstonecraft Godwin) 4, 5, 8, 9, 14, 16, 18, 20, 21, 22, 23, 24, 25, 26, 27
Shelley, Percy Bysshe 5, 8, 24
South Africa 25
St. Petersburg 6
sublime nature 16, 17
symbolism 9, 10, 15, 18, 19, 28

theme 15, 16, 17, 18, 28

values 16

Walton, Robert 6, 7, 12, 13, 19, 21
Wollstonecraft, Mary 4

Young Frankenstein 24

LIGHTBOX

SUPPLEMENTARY RESOURCES

Click on the plus icon found in the bottom left corner of each spread to open additional teacher resources.

- Download and print the book's quizzes and activities
- Access curriculum correlations
- Explore additional web applications that enhance the Lightbox experience

LIGHTBOX DIGITAL TITLES

Packed full of integrated media

VIDEOS

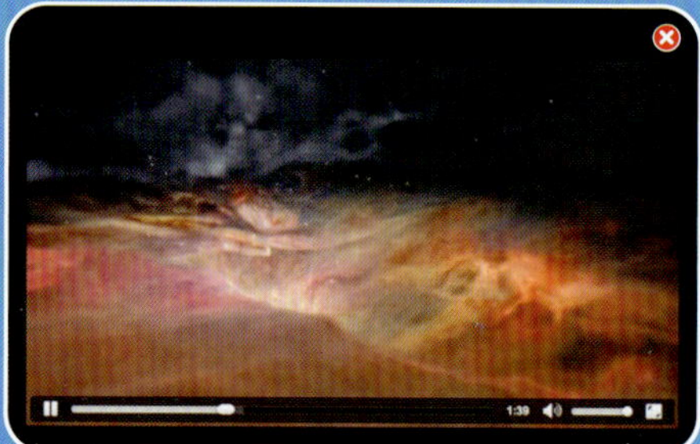

INTERACTIVE MAPS

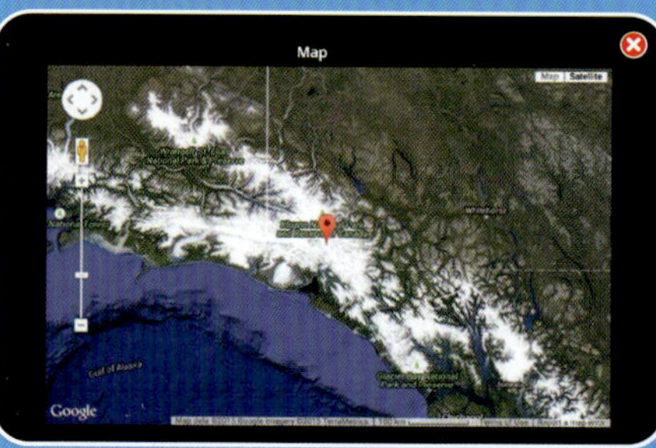

WEBLINKS

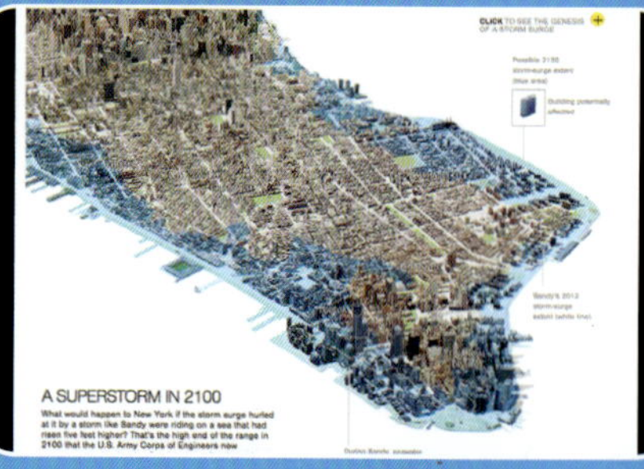

SLIDESHOWS

QUIZZES

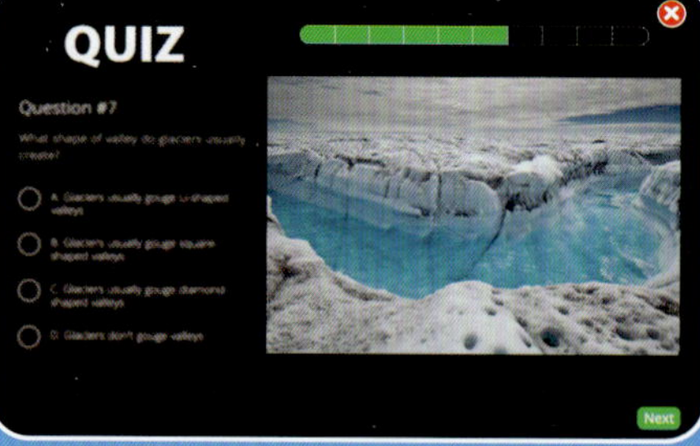

OPTIMIZED FOR

- ✔ TABLETS
- ✔ SMART BOARDS
- ✔ COMPUTERS
- ✔ AND MUCH MORE!

Published by Lightbox Learning Inc.
276 5th Avenue, Suite 704 #917 New York, NY 10118
www.openlightbox.com

Library of Congress Control Number: 2024941738

ISBN 978-1-5105-8410-5 (hardcover)
ISBN 978-1-5105-8411-2 (static multi-user eBook)
ISBN 978-1-5105-8413-6 (interactive multi-user eBook)

Printed in Guangzhou, China
1 2 3 4 5 6 7 8 9 0 28 27 26 25 24

072024
111423

Project Coordinator: John Willis
Art Director: Terry Paulhus
Layout: Jean Faye Rodriguez

Every reasonable effort has been made to trace ownership and to obtain permission to reprint copyright material. The publisher would be pleased to have any errors or omissions brought to its attention so that they may be corrected in subsequent printings. The publisher acknowledges Alamy, Getty Images, Shutterstock, and Wikimedia as its primary image suppliers for this title.